Five years of seasons

by

Phil Santus

First published 2023 by The Hedgehog Poetry Press,

5 Coppack House, Churchill Avenue, Clevedon. BS21 6QW

www.hedgehogpress.co.uk

Copyright © Phil Santus 2023

ISBN: 978-1-916830-09-7

Contents

Spring 1: 5

Summer 1: 6

Autumn 1: 7

Winter 1: 8

Spring 2: 9

Summer 2: 10

Autumn 2: 11

Winter 2: 12

Spring 3: 13

Summer 3: 14

Autumn 3: 15

Winter 3: 16

Spring 4: 17

Summer 4: 18

Autumn 4 19

Winter 4: 20

Spring 5: 21

Summer 5: 22

Autumn 5: 23

Winter 5: 24

SPRING 1:

<u>The frost meadow</u>

Spring is harsh this year.
Frost glistens on fields and trees,
and life has to wait.

The silent air hints
at hibernation or death,
and unsettles me.

I am divorced from
Nature's sheer brutality.
I am privileged.

My boots leave footprints
on the whitened frost meadow.
Soon they will be gone.

SUMMER 1:

What used to be

The glad summer clouds,
sit arrayed in hazy skies,
far and expansive.

Bright sunlight filters
through the canopy of leaves,
an evocation

of lost childhood days,
when happiness was simply
a run and a climb.

I feel it dimly,
as a half-forgotten glimpse
of what used to be.

AUTUMN 1:

<u>First term</u>

Autumn awakens
old longings and ambitions,
brings me beginnings.

These halls of learning
echo with conversation,
waiting on knowledge

that will liberate
and will skill the future years.
Our youth is passing.

Life is not easy,
and age will have its regrets,
hidden from the young.

WINTER 1:

<u>Old age</u>

My legs refuse me.
Lying upon the cold tiles,
I know its winter.

Here it was I fell.
It was yesterday, I think,
and here I remain.

My wife steps over,
doesn't think to call for help,
but offers me tea.

We both have issues.
Dementia's a sad disease.
My breath gets wheezy.

SPRING 2:

<u>Alaska by satellite</u>

Swirls of plankton bloom,
off the coast of Alaska,
viewed from outer space.

Plankton feeds the chain
(fish, sea lions, killer whales),
fuelled by the sun.

Plankton and the trees,
living lungs of the planet,
keeping us alive.

Ice sheets warm and melt,
and rivers are unfrozen,
brimming with new life.

SUMMER 2:

<u>Wish you were here</u>

Summer is joyful.
I can cherish longer days
and can breathe freely.

Recovery is
a simple process of light,
sea air and freedom.

My thoughts are restored
and I find myself at peace,
better than before.

You should see the waves
as they crash upon the shore.
I wish you were here.

AUTUMN 2:

<u>Harvest festival</u>

We must be grateful
for all the things around us,
things we might destroy.

The forests of Earth
and oceans and the pastures
cradle us with life.

If the insects go,
are poisoned to extinction,
nothing will survive.

Think of this during
the full moon in September,
blessing the harvest.

WINTER 2:

Winter will be gone

I tried not to tell.
You were desperate for time
to put things aright.

Secrets have a way
to spill in conversation.
It wasn't my fault.

So I gave them this,
an insight and a knowledge,
think it's for the best.

If you can confront
your worst fears and your actions,
winter will be gone.

SPRING 3:

<u>Spring flowers</u>

Crocus and snowdrop
bloom through days of snow and frost,
rising with the spring.

Winter aconite
spreads out beneath witch hazel,
a gardener's dream.

Roadside daffodils,
clusters of yellow glory,
well done the council.

Acres of bluebells,
blue vistas of broken light,
in ancient woodland.

SUMMER 3:

<u>The puzzle of its existence</u>

I love this flower,
for it is other-worldly,
it is transcendent.

Its earth is sacred.
Its petals know distant suns
provide its succour.

No insect visits.
It is born to die untouched,
and will not return.

It has its reasons,
beyond imagination,
and improbable.

AUTUMN 3:

<u>The web</u>

Sunlight and shadow
contrast on the spider's web,
cradled in the tree.

It has a beauty
in its perfect symmetry,
captured by the sun.

Its shining structure
belies its ugly purpose,
the taking of life.

It recalls to me
human ingenuity
in the art of war.

WINTER 3:

<u>Winter has moments</u>

Winter has moments
of loveliness and splendour,
its days of grandeur.

Here is a meadow,
fronting a leaf-bare woodland,
stark against the sky.

The wooden lychgate
of a medieval church,
laden full with snow.

The winter sunshine,
sparkling upon the water,
bright on icy streams.

SPRING 4:

<u>Death nurtures life</u>

I can't explain why,
there are so many reasons,
too many to tell.

Did you expect this,
that the parting of the ways
could be so easy?

It has a logic,
and you show no bitterness,
no hint of regret.

We had our moments.
Spring is an awakening
and death nurtures life.

SUMMER 4:

<u>A sunny day</u>

I do not want it.
This glorious day rankles,
and leaves me bereft.

Failure presses me
with thoughts of desolation,
knowing it's too late.

I think of options,
the paths I could have chosen,
open then, now closed.

This sun-soaked landscape
is resonant with beauty,
spoiled by my regrets.

AUTUMN 4

The politician's fantasy

I am not ready
to relinquish my power
on this autumn day.

My ministers speak
of duty and sacrifice,
but I disagree.

I will continue
and will be vindicated
by my legacy.

When the time has come,
I will leave on my own terms,
and be proven right.

WINTER 4:

<u>My boys</u>

My boys love conkers.
They collect and cherish them
like finest treasures.

My boys love snowfall.
I hear their squeals of laughter.
They make me happy.

My boys love climbing.
Sometimes I am scared for them,
but I let them climb.

My boys are hopeful,
and, for them, life has wonder.
I could learn from them.

SPRING 5:

<u>Distant horizons</u>

Distant horizons
are metaphors for a life,
holding a promise

of far tomorrows,
of the unexplored country,
or yearned-for solace.

They are the lost days
of our childhood memories
and contented bliss

or the harbingers
of new experiences
and vivid living.

SUMMER 5:

<u>Nightingale</u>

The sweet nightingale,
from atop the silver branch,
sings a pretty tune.

The muse of poets,
of Homer, Shakespeare and Keats,
sings a sad lament,

or expresses joy,
depending on whom listens
and their state of mind.

The voice of nature,
in truth, is a single male
singing for a mate.

AUTUMN 5:

Earth seen from the space station

Circled by starlight,
the wide glory of this Earth
can be viewed from here.

The blue of oceans,
greens and browns of continents,
contrasts and wonders.

From this high platform,
the cares of humanity
are distant from me.

The Caribbean,
the eye of the hurricane,
beautiful from here.

WINTER 5:

Legacy

If I gave to you
a legacy of stories,
they would become yours.

Tales of adventure,
of larks and discovery,
they would enrich you.

You are my children
and I am responsible
for your wanderings,

so I'll give to you
a legacy of stories,
they will become yours.